Animal
Defences

THIS EDITION
Editorial Management by Oriel Square
Produced for DK by WonderLab Group LLC
Jennifer Emmett, Erica Green, Kate Hale, *Founders*

Editors Grace Hill Smith, Libby Romero, Maya Myers, Michaela Weglinski;
Photography Editors Kelley Miller, Annette Kiesow, Nicole di Mella; **Managing Editor** Rachel Houghton;
Designers Project Design Company; **Researcher** Michelle Harris; **Copy Editor** Lori Merritt;
Indexer Connie Binder; **Proofreader** Larry Shea; **Reading Specialist** Dr. Jennifer Albro;
Curriculum Specialist Elaine Larson

Published in Great Britain by Dorling Kindersley Limited
DK, One Embassy Gardens, 8 Viaduct Gardens, London, SW11 7BW

The authorised representative in the EEA is
Dorling Kindersley Verlag GmbH. Arnulfstr. 124,
80636 Munich, Germany

Copyright © 2023 Dorling Kindersley Limited
A Penguin Random House Company
10 9 8 7 6 5 4 3 2 1
001–334100–July/2023

A catalogue record for this book
is available from the British Library.
ISBN: 978-0-2416-0270-6

Printed and bound in China

The publisher would like to thank the following for their kind permission to reproduce their images:
a=above; c=centre; b=below; l=left; r=right; t=top; b/g=background

Alamy Stock Photo: Nature Picture Library / Alex Mustard 14bl, Panoramic Images 3cb, SBS Eclectic Images 13tr,
Poelzer Wolfgang 23tr; **Dreamstime.com:** Agami Photo Agency 18br, Belizar 17c, Vicky Chauhan 16–17, Eastmanphoto 1b,
Farinoza 30cb, David Havel 28l, Olga Khoroshunova 25bl, Klomsky 15tr, Voislav Kolevski 27, Carlos Soler Martinez 11,
Steven Melanson / Xscream1 6cl, Oksanavg 11tr, Jason Ondreicka 6–7b, 10br, Samfoto 8–9, Seth Schubert 22b, David Steele 14–15,
Kasira Suda 21br, Baramee Temboonkiat 29t, Vaclav Volrab 12b; **Getty Images:** Moment / Jared Lloyd 18tr,
Moment / Stan Tekiela Author / Naturalist / Wildlife Photographer 20br, Photographer's Choice RF / Sylvain Cordier 8cl,
Stone / Paul Starosta 23br, The Image Bank / Mark Newman 7cr; **Getty Images / iStock:** 2630ben 4–5, Mark Alexander 25tr,
lilithlita 13crb, nattanan726 24; **naturepl.com:** Klein & Hubert 18–19, Nature Production 21c, Gary Bell / Oceanwide 26crb;
Shutterstock.com: Rob Jansen 17crb, Reimar 8br

Cover images: *Front:* **Getty Images / iStock:** Lynn_Bystrom; *Back:* **Dreamstime.com:** Gerald Deboer cla, Eastmanphoto cra

All other images © Dorling Kindersley
For more information see: www.dkimages.com

For the curious
www.dk.com

Animal Defences

Ruth A. Musgrave

Contents

A Good Defence

Stingers, poison, spines even a little vomit! Defences like these help animals to survive.

Animals need to find food and mates and take care of their babies. They do all that while avoiding predators, or animals that want to eat them.

Sea Stings

Jellyfish, sea anemones and coral are related. They all have tiny, venomous stingers that protect them and help them to catch food.

poison dart frog

Prey have amazing defences to stop bigger, stronger predators in their tracks. No defence is foolproof, but a good one gives prey a chance to escape. Let's take a look at some astonishing animal defences.

How Stunning!
An electric eel shocks its predators. The jolt is higher than that of an electrical socket.

A Great Cover-Up

Blending in is one of the most common defences.

It's a bird. Or is it a tree? This bird sleeps in trees during the day. Its feathers match the tree bark. The bird holds its body just right. Now, it is hard to tell where the tree ends and the bird begins.

**great potoo
and chick**

No Rush
Sloths move so slowly that algae grow in their fur. Life in slow motion is a great defence for these tree dwellers. Algae help them to blend in with the trees' green leaves.

Some animals can change colour with the seasons. In the summer, the arctic hare's brown fur blends in with plants and rocks. In late autumn, white fur begins to replace the brown fur. The hare will stay hidden in the winter snow from predators like foxes and wolves.

arctic hare

The Great Pretenders

Some animals take blending in to the next level. They look and act like something completely different.

Stick insects look like sticks and leaves. They even sway in the breeze like plants. A hungry predator will go straight past.

Stick insects can protect themselves even before they hatch. Their eggs look like seeds that ants eat. Ants take the eggs back to their nest. They eat part of the outside of the eggs. The ants drop the rest of the egg. The baby stick insect then grows and hatches in the safety of the ant nest.

Toxic Twin
The harmless scarlet king snake's colours look like those of a venomous coral snake. Predators steer clear of both kinds of snakes.

Plant Protection
A frogfish can change its colour to look like coral and rocks on the seafloor.

stick insect

Poisonous and Venomous

Predators avoid poisonous and venomous animals. Poisonous animals share their toxins when a predator tries to touch or eat them. Venomous animals deliver their toxins by biting, stinging or spraying.

A golden poison frog's skin oozes a deadly toxin. The bright yellow colour of this tiny frog warns predators to stay away. But if they try to eat the frog, they will quickly die. A golden poison frog has enough poison to kill 20,000 mice. Scientists think that these frogs get their poison from the insects they eat.

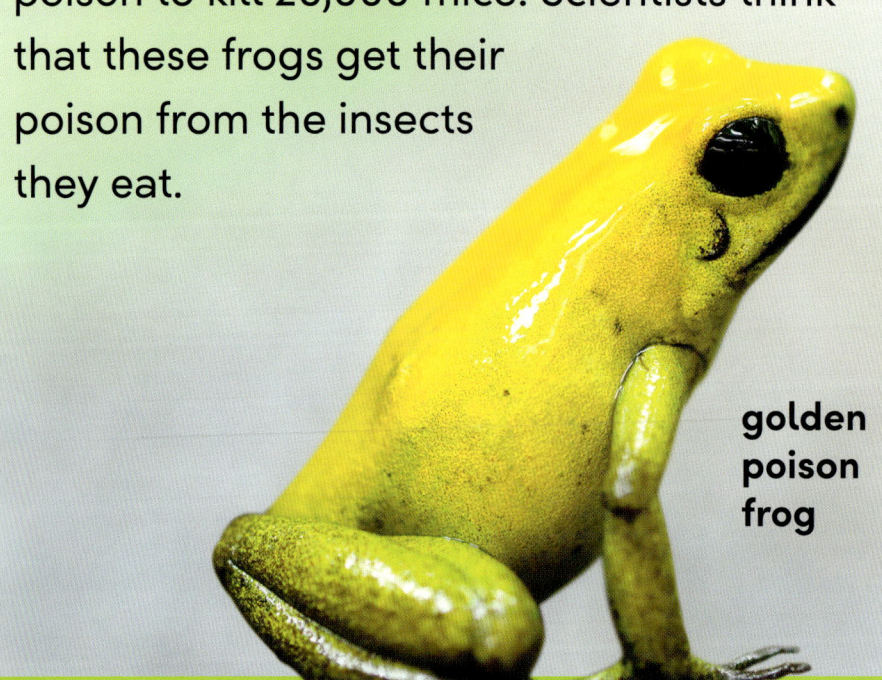

golden poison frog

The African crested rat doesn't make its own poison either. It chews the toxic bark and roots of the arrow-poison tree. Then, it transfers the  toxins by licking its own special hairs that soak up the poison. An animal that grabs the rat gets a poisonous mouthful.

venomous spines

Dangerous Beauty
The lionfish's fins are beautiful but deadly. The tips are armed with sharp, venomous spines.

Bigger Is Better

When it comes to stopping a predator, size is a safeguard. For example, few animals try to hunt African elephants. They are nearly as tall as a double-decker bus. Elephants also stop predators by staying together. Elephants live in herds. If a predator tries to attack, it risks being trampled by one or more elephants that weigh as much as two ice-cream vans.

Supersized
No predator is even close to the size of the world's largest animal, the blue whale. It can be longer than three buses. Its tongue alone weighs as much as an elephant!

Like elephants, hippos have size on their side, too. A large male hippo weighs as much as nine horses. These enormous  animals have giant teeth as long as a child's arm. Their bite can kill a crocodile.

Amazing Armour

How else does an animal defend itself against the teeth and claws of a lion or cougar? Armour!

Sharp, hard scales cover the pangolin's body. The pangolin curls into a ball if a lion or other predator tries to eat it. This roly-poly move protects its underside, which does not have scales. The pangolin can even roll away.

pangolin

Armadillos have armour, too. Their shell protects their back. Some armadillos flatten themselves on the ground to protect their soft underbelly. The three-banded armadillo rolls into a ball. It tucks itself completely inside its shell. Sometimes, it leaves the shell open just a bit. If the predator sticks a paw inside ... snap! The armadillo closes the shell to pinch the predator's paw.

armadillo

Surprise Getaway

For many animals, survival depends on escaping or evading predators as quickly as possible.

Pronghorn live on open, flat grasslands where there are few places to hide. But speed is their defence. Pronghorn can run at more than 80 kilometres per hour. Their excellent eyesight also allows these animals to spot predators from far away. That makes it hard for animals like coyotes and bobcats to even get close to a pronghorn herd.

Fins for the Win

Flying fish leap out of the water to avoid predators like tuna, swordfish and sea lions. They spread their wide fins and glide across the ocean's surface.

Quick jumps can help animals to evade predators, too. The jerboa leaps like a kangaroo to escape predators like foxes and snakes. Long legs and big feet help it to jump more than a car length at a time. It can quickly change direction with every jump. That makes it harder for a hungry hunter to know which way to run.

jerboa

Spray Away!

Some animals spray to warn predators to stay away. When threatened, skunks shoot out a spray that keeps predators like coyotes and cougars at a distance. The smelly spray can burn their eyes. The spotted skunk's warning starts with a handstand. Then, it spreads its hind legs and fans out its tail. If this display doesn't work, the skunk takes aim. It squirts spray from glands near its tail. It hits the predator with amazing accuracy.

Like skunks, one type of beetle sprays from its back end. But the spray from this tiny beetle packs a more powerful punch.

The bombardier beetle stores two chemicals in its abdomen. The beetle mixes and then releases these chemicals when predators like ants, toads or birds get too close. This almost boiling liquid is hot enough to burn human skin.

bombardier beetle

Unstoppable

In one study, about half the toads that swallowed these beetles vomited them up. The beetles were still alive and energetic.

Defensive Distractions

Animals use different ways to distract predators. That gives prey a chance to escape.

Losing body parts is a great defence found on land and in the sea. For example, the bright blue tail of this skink attracts a predator to the tail rather than the head. That gives the skink a chance to drop its tail and scurry away. The predator is then left with just the tail.

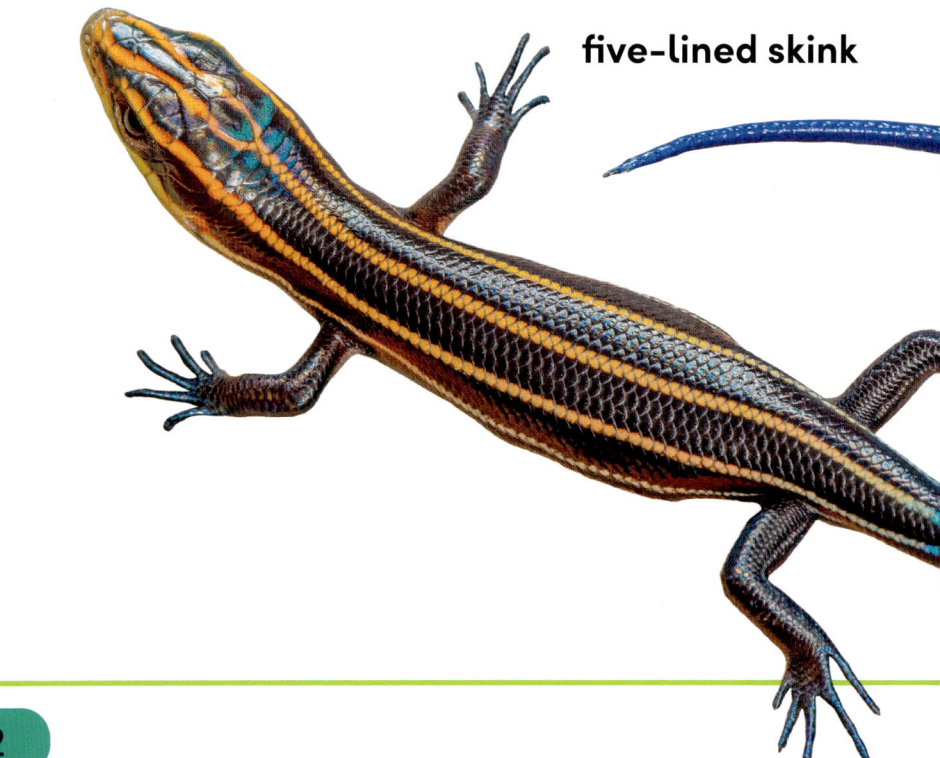

five-lined skink

Some sea cucumbers shoot out their internal organs. The predator attacks the dropped body parts, and the sea cucumber scoots away. The body parts that the sea cucumber dropped grow back.

Claws Out!
When attacked, the hairy frog flexes muscles in its hind legs. This motion breaks the tips of the bones in its toes. The broken bones pierce the skin and create claws.

Teamwork

Meerkats live in large groups in burrows. These animals work as a team to find food, take care of their babies and protect each other. Some of them stand guard above their underground homes to watch for danger. They call a loud warning if a deadly snake approaches. The meerkats then work together to surround the snake.

American bison find safety in numbers, too. The herd works together to make it harder for wolves or grizzly bears to attack one of them. A bison's size, strength and deadly horns can keep a predator from coming close.

Tentacle Teamwork

Clownfish and sea anemones team up for protection. The anemone keeps the clownfish safe from predators. In return, the clownfish cleans the anemone's tentacles and chases away fish that try to eat the anemone.

Stealing to Survive

For some prey, the best defence is another animal's.

A nudibranch eats sea anemones. Anemones have stinging cells in their tentacles. The nudibranch covers the anemone's stingers with slime to turn it into a painless meal. It swallows and stores the stingers in its guts. If attacked, the nudibranch shoots the stingers at predators.

The pom-pom crab steals a sea anemone's painful stings, too. But instead of eating the anemone, the crab carries one in each of its claws. It waves the colourful creature's tentacles to warn off predators. When directly threatened, the crab thrusts the anemones forward with a protective punch.

pom-pom crab

nudibranch

Saved by Slime

Some animals use slime to protect themselves.

Many bird chicks are helpless when their parents leave the nest to find food. But European roller chicks have a helpful defence. They vomit a stinky orange goo if a predator grabs or touches them. Chicks can release this liquid even before their eyes open. The vomit is also a warning to the chicks' parents that a predator might be nearby.

Mandarinfish use stinky slime as a defence, too. They do not have protective scales like many fish. Instead, a thick, stinky, poisonous slime coats their skin. The fish's bright colours warn predators to stay away, but if a predator does try to take a bite, it will get a mouthful of some nasty-tasting stuff!

Using their strength, size, spray or slime, or by hiding in plain sight, animals have many ways to protect themselves. Which is the best defence? The one that works!

Glossary

Burrow
A tunnel dug underground where animals live and hide

Nudibranch
A relative of snails that does not have a shell

Poisonous
Animals that often release toxins through their skin when another animal tries to touch or eat them

Predator
An animal that eats other animals

Prey
Animals that predators eat

Toxin
A poison or venom created by a plant or animal

Venomous
Animals that often share their toxins by biting, stinging or spraying

Index

Quiz

Answer the questions to see what you have learnt. Check your answers in the key below.

1. What animal's fur changes colour with the seasons?

2. What do the golden poison frog and the African crested rat have in common?

3. Which two land animals use teamwork as a defence?

4. How does a five-lined skink startle predators?

5. What does a pom-pom crab use for protection?

6. What animal leaps like a kangaroo to evade predators?

7. How do European roller chicks protect themselves from predators?

8. True or False: Mandarinfish have scales like other fish.

1. Arctic hare 2. They are both poisonous
3. Meerkats and American bison 4. It drops its tail 5. Sea anemones
6. Jerboa 7. They vomit a stinky orange goo 8. False